CHOOSING THE ROUTE

Patrick B. Osada

Indigo Dreams Publishing

First Edition: Choosing The Route

First published in Great Britain in 2010 by:
Indigo Dreams Publishing
132 Hinckley Road
Stoney Stanton
Leics
LE9 4LN

www.indigodreams.co.uk

Patrick B. Osada has asserted his right under the Copyright, Designs and Patents Act 1988 to be identified as the author of this work.
©2010 Patrick B. Osada

ISBN 978-1-907401-13-8

British Library Cataloguing in Publication Data. A CIP record for this book can be obtained from the British Library.

Designed and typeset in Baskerville Old Face and Times New Roman by Indigo Dreams.

Cover photograph by Brent Jones.

Printed and bound in Great Britain by Imprint Academic, Exeter.

For my own compass and sheet anchor...

Acknowledgements:

Twenty of the poems in this collection have appeared in the following Magazines and websites:

Acumen, Cylamens & Swords, HQ Magazine, Other Poetry, Other Voices, Poetry Cornwall, Poetry Monthly international, Reach Poetry, SOUTH Poetry Magazine, The Gloucester Citizen, The Great War Magazine, The Interpreter's House, The Poetry Kit (Featured Poet - Caught in the Net), Voices Israel Anthology 2009.

Visiting and *Dark* were highly commended in the ORTA Poetry on the Lake Competition 2010.

Previous Collections:

Close to the Edge
Short Stories: Suburban Lives
Rough Music

CONTENTS

CHOOSING THE ROUTE

A Collection Of New Poems

Patrick B. Osada

"The journey is the reward" Ancient Chinese Proverb

From Route 47

On my bus ticket
There is space enough to write
This tiny poem.

FORCE of NATURE

Whoosh! Like a force of nature they arrive...
Starlings. This boisterous, squawking, noisy mob,
 strutting, uncouth gang, intimidate all
cautious birds : dunnocks, chaffinch, secret wrens.

Spreading across the feeding site, they clear
spilt grain, steal perches from the smaller birds.
Clumsily they ride the feeder's wild swing –
scattering seed on hooligans below,
stabbing at brave sparrows, bluetits, finches
whose presence threatens to disrupt the show.

Leaving as quickly as they came, this flock-
of-one-mind swarms a laden apple tree
to ruin near-ripe fruit with casual pecks.
Then off again, a ragged hurtling mass,
to pounce on fields, string power lines like beads.

At day's close they rise as one: this wheeling,
darkling flock shape-shifts in a setting sun.
Across the land a ritual soon repeats:
sharing a common pulse they turn, turn again,
flocks swoop fields, skirt factories, circle streets
as they follow weird tracks through empty air –
invisible to all but these strange birds.

At old Bisham two golfers have to wait
as starlings drive the fairway of the eighth;
like swarming bees they funnel single file,
descend upon an ivy-covered trunk
to disappear completely – swallowed up...
Creating, from a tree and avian clan,
a trembling, cackling sight of the Green Man.

REFUGEES

Escaping gunfire from the sea,
fear and blind panic drove them on
like any other refugees.
Without the loadstar of their lives,
away from the familiar,
they travelled unseen through the night
from far beyond the ocean's swell.

Singing, to keep their spirits high,
they passed Black Rock and Castle Point
to swing into the broad Porthcuel...
Beyond moored boats with jangling sheets,
the sleeping Manor House at Place,
they lost their way and chose Porth Creek.

Into this elemental place
of mudflats, long abandoned boats,
they moved in on a changing tide.
Beneath the overhanging oaks
where brown stream narrows, up near Froe,
the tidal waters ebbed away.

Caught up in flotsam, debris, weed,
the party floundered in the creek
as channel water turned to shoals.
The sun rose on the carnage there,
as gardeners raised the alarm –
of those who travelled from the sea,
only a handful still survived.

Now mouths are stopped – their chant has gone
and eyes are blind to helping hands
as men humped bodies to the grass.
There's tragedy, no respite won,
no refuge in this hostile land –
for those who've journeyed from so far
the sole lament is curlews' song.

On June 9ᵗʰ 2008 a large pod of dolphins was discovered beached in the shallows of Porth Creek, Cornwall – 26 had died. It is believed that they had been panicked by explosions in Falmouth Bay during a naval exercise.

RISUS SARDONICUS

Clamouring Sunday bells. The shimmering air,
Iridescent mirror of a brassy sun,
Conducts the peals across the dew decked lawn
To drone, petal soft amongst the bees,
Or climb, conspiring with birds in song.

Wandering the dusty greyness of the path
I linger, cool amongst trim green of yew,
And from refreshing shade imagine,
Above the distant jangling bells,
The hollyhocks, brazen, trumpeting the day.

Beyond the yews the dappled shade of pine extends.
The trees, a cool and peaceful nave,
Inviolable against the glaring day,
Command a quieting of mind, composure,
Peace within this sanctuary.

Vaulting pine fronds screen a darkling sun
Spreading the light as gleaming pools of gold:
Adorning trifles.
                    A gilded fir cone attracts my eye,
                    Auspicious blood berries lie close by.

Here decaying leaves are speckled red,
The splattered blood has left a natural trail
Too visible to ignore....... I follow,
Scuffing silence. Steps rasp fallen leaves -
My cautious progress amplified.

Beneath a bush I find him lying,
Unnatural, twisted, posturing in death:
Defiance frozen in his reaching limbs,
Anguish smiles crookedly through bared teeth,
Eyes fixed, a final glare of grief.

Hypnotized by death I stand transfixed
Till suddenly the silence roars with bells.
Trembling, white faced, I hurry into church,
Small boy haunted by a fox's death -
I daren't look at the crucifix.

SEEING THINGS

Close by the bridge, at Spencer's church,
a red cross flutters in the breeze;
first swallows turn above the Thames
where swan flotilla glides downstream.

A solitary boat drifts on;
two walkers, with a map and dog,
seem set to walk on to Bourne End,
leaving behind a crow and thoughts...

Perched on a rotting willow trunk,
nodding and bowing to the stream,
he seems to concentrate so hard
watching the water's glassy sheen.

Then, suddenly, he takes to flight –
matching his wing beats to the breeze,
he seems to hover in the air
and touch the tops of waves mid-stream

to snatch from waters some small prey.
Retiring to the other bank,
he eats his meal in privacy
before returning to his tree.

Twice more this fishing crow performs
then flies off to a distant oak –
leaving in mind a miracle:
a memory, a puff of smoke.

THE VEERY BIRD
(Catharus Fuscesceus)

It was the twittering that brought them here,
texts, blogs, directions on a birder's site.
Along the road they came in droves: same clothes –
their colours uniform, all browns and green –
same team supporters, late for their big match.

And locals joined in too: small boys on bikes,
men with hoes, abandoned their allotments
to lean on gates and watch these *twitchers* pass;
even young lovers marry with the queue:
desire now focussed on a migrant bird.

Labouring at the rear, a fat man sweats
in camouflage, long lenses ready set
to catch history if he's not too late...

But late he was – murder was committed:
he missed the bird, snapped the cat who did it.

"Rare bird flew from US to be eaten by a cat" - **Daily Record**

CHANGES (Autumn Dawn)

In a sliver of burnished light
Sad hostas turn to yellow lace,
Spent chestnut leaves begin to fall
As distant woods unpick the night.

Far *matins* chimes fall on the ear,
Notes fade to memory like days...
As seconds pass the season runs
And life moves on like Earth round Sun.

FOREST ROAD

It was his chosen route:
cross-country, climb with views;
after weeks of non-stop work
a ride was overdue.

Half way up Cabbage Hill
the big oak spread its shade,
here a lone thin buzzard sat –
eked out stark winter days.

One cold December night,
when trapped in headlamps' blaze,
a slight deer leapt this frozen ditch
to safety in dark fields.

Today in muggy heat
weekend's thin traffic slows,
forms into a sudden queue –
blue lights along the road.

Dark figures in the shade –
a twisted bike retrieved;
medics find their way too late
to give essential aid.

CHAIN FLAIL

With careless ease, in half an hour,
this driver, tractor and chain flail
will decimate our lane's rich hedge
and recreate the shell torn Somme.

Young trees are left as limbless stumps,
lopped branches, splintered, on the ground
and all the way across the lane,
confetti made from this year's buds.

Yet here, only a field away,
a proper hedge is taking shape.
One man with skill and simple tools
creates a hedge to last for life.

A swift, low cut pleaches young trees,
he weaves them between hazel stakes
to make a kind of basketwork
of living growth, shapely and tight.

Such skilful work always takes time:
to plash a hedge, stock-proof and strong,
is costed out in yards a day –
the time it takes to get it right.

The tractor man and his blunt flail?
He'll tear and lop a hedge to shape,
makes no repairs where stock may stray
but always clocks the miles up...

So, where have all the experts gone
who'd lay a hedge and clear a ditch?
Replaced by men who drive machines –
That way contractors end up rich.

CLIVEDEN in NOVEMBER

No breath of wind to stir the morning mist,
trouble fallen leaves or grasses' fragileness.
Red maple flares - reflected in dark pool,
no birds to sing, now all around is still.

Briefly, low sun illuminates the scene:
touching late berries by the water's lip
where elephant-grey gunnera decays...
Quite motionless, the languid heron sits.

From gilded fish above the Chinese room
and on, passed house and parterre to the Thames;
from orangery, with blaze of pink nerines,
and algae covered statues in the trees.

It is as if the world has held its breath:
this moment set forever by stilled time,
as in amber, or a bubble, beauty rests –
until the spell was broken by a chime...

Somewhere a muntjac barked, a chainsaw buzzed...
and, in the big house, staff prepared for lunch.
Then, like an after-thought, a robin sang
prompting hushed birds, *"Come join in joyous song!"*

AT PEGGY'S PLACE

Where Peacock and "beloved babes"
Had yapped and scampered in the sun,
A tabby strolls near Moore's small form,
Jumps up on Peggy's marble throne
To sit and groom and lick her paws.

Only the bells disturb us here
Near Giacommetti's hopping man
Beneath high trees, in welcome shade,
A blackbird flashes down the path
Where legend claims a lion played.

Inside, where once the Ballets Rousses
Had come to stay and strut their stuff,
Calder's strange petals twirl to fall.
His bed head's there but not the bed –
There is a couch from Peggy's days,
But now it's ART that's centre stage.

"Il Palazzo Nonfinito" –
A gallery, no longer home –
Has lost her spirit, kept her ART...
But how it shines! – She would be pleased
Picasso, Braque and all the rest
Engaged in ways that she had known –
Such dreams and visions caught in paint.

But constantly the eye is drawn
Towards a work un-catalogued –
A Caneletto never framed
Except by windows and the door...

And from the terrace, arms aloft,
The hard-on Angel so exults
The city view he overlooks
You half expect to hear him shout.

In 1949 Peggy Guggenheim bought the unfinished 18th Century "Palazzo Venier dei Lioni" as her Venice home. She lived there for 30 years whilst assembling a world famous collection of modern painting and sculpture.On the terrace, overlooking the Grand Canal, stands Marini's "Angelo della Citta" – a naked equestrian figure, erect in all respects.

AT THE ACCADEMIA

Joining the quest, queuing for hours...
passed hawkers with their replicas,
buskers, beggars, picture sellers
beside the grim graffitied walls.

Inside, we pass Renaissance art –
crammed on high walls it's hard to see –
given just a cursory glance
by tourist crowds anxious to reach
the icon that has drawn them here.

The mass moves on, oblivious
to *prisoners* trapped in the stone –
those *slaves* of Michelangelo,
huge forms he failed to *liberate* –
it's David that they're here to see.

In an alcove 'specially built,
we look up at that gangly youth,
carved from a block da Vinci scorned.
A hand seems large, the neck too long,
that famous manhood rather small :
proportion changes with the view -
he's best seen close to, from below...

For many, David ticks that box:
Places to Go or *Things to See* –
a quick trip round his pedestal
then out, to buy a souvenir.

Beside the statue, a huge screen
provides us with a 3-D view.
With games-machine-like hand controls
the image can be made to twist,
revealing detail rarely seen:
views from above, inside of wrist,
a close-up of those famous lips...

Aware of this, bored teenagers
soon spot a chance to have a laugh –
their pleasure breaks the silence here
as, deftly, they make David dance.

VISITING

Do ghosts still recognise this town?
The layout of the road's unchanged –
but buildings here are roofless now,
taverns inhospitable.

Tourists with guidebooks jam Pompeii:
as busy as that far off day
when crowds were toasting *Jupiter* –
surprising that this place remains...

Empty buildings, stripped to the bone
retain the irremovable:
an intricate mosaic floor
confirms this was a rich man's home

sign writing marks some old shop fronts
and everywhere, on many walls,
are colours from those far off days.
Paintings of gods, birds, animals –

small areas of vivid paint –
display their lives : the everyday.
Set like a photographic plate,
here on this wall, a face stares out

with bulging eyes contorted mouth –
real terror stares across the years
as if the person were transfixed,
caught in a moment, turned to stone...

by gorgon of the mountainside:
come visiting this woman's home.

LAMENT FOR GLOUCESTER

Transformed in only forty years!
The fading dowager I'd known
Who lounged close by the Severn's side
Has almost vanished, lost to time.
And in her place, near by-pass roads,
In cheap shell-suit and thrift shop dross,
A sad bag lady stops to squat.

Once famed for parliament of kings,
The place that changed the Civil War,
Finds infamy through recent sons:
A terrorist, depraved Fred West.
So where has *England's Glory* gone?
The cachet of a market town
Where shoppers came from miles around
By coach from Wales and the South West.

Lost heritage is what we find –
A cheapness and a dumbing-down –
The old Guildhall become a bank,
A row of Tudor buildings gone,
Blackfriars lost beneath used tyres,
The place to view the Eastgate walls
Is perch for dossers, dead-eyed kids.

And so the City's face has changed:
The nip and tuck of poor design
Creates a mess of many styles
Largely bereft of charm or age.
Above it all Cathedral towers
Watching new suburbs stretch towards
Blue hills: engulfing countryside.

VISITING INDIA: A Poetry Sequence

ARRIVAL

Marvel at the light,
Saris bright as butterflies,
Traffic and the heat.

TOURIST HOTEL

Heat so pervasive
Makes you sweat in the shower,
Big fans slice thick air.

WONDER

Seen from the river
White Taj Mahal shimmers, floats –
Mirage in the sun.

VILLAGE

Monkeys everywhere.
Like children, up to no good,
Leap from roof to roof.

PHOTOGRAPH WITH BANANAS

Wearing a monkey
Like a Davy Crockett hat –
Holiday highlight.

SURPRISE

Hindu swastikas
Decorate the temple walls –
Surprise western eyes.

MONSOON

An uneasy truce:
Day breaks with red in its eye –
It'll not stay dry.

Waking in the night
The rain has a thousand sounds –
Today it's drumming.

AT THE RAILWAY STATION

Ignored by the crowd
Stepping round this pile of rags –
Dead beggars don't count.

EVENING

Brilliant sunset:
Blood-orange sun slips away,
Leaving amber sky.

OUT OF AFRICA

Swifts turn and call above the Alhambra:
tent like palaces with slim marble poles,
honeycombed ceilings charm all cameras –
reflected in water where tourists stroll.
Climbing burnished air, these dark scimitars
swoop the cooling fountains where Nasrids sipped;
led the Moors to Spain, out of Africa,
tracing burning skies with Arabic script.

Links to bygone age and Muslim conquests –
swifts still nest today on Sabika Hill.
A few led the way to England's northwest,
a strange paradise where the air is chill...
There's no palace here for modern pilgrims –
plastic minarets that a lone swift skims

MORE HOME THOUGHTS FROM ABROAD

Outside the airport, waiting for the bus.
Sauna heat, such air, so damp and thick
I must grow gills to breathe.
Driving into dusk and sudden dark:
Thunderheads mass as neon flares,
Forked lightning strobes the sky.

Sleepless, I ride air conditioned drone
Just like my ten hour flight:
My body says it's breakfast time -
Here it's still the middle of the night.

As light begins to fill this motel room,
I watch dawn break across an alien land:
Strange trees; buildings, unrecognizable
From shadows I first knew, disclose
Themselves in startling shapes and hues.

And, through a veil of tiredness it's plain
That I have travelled all those miles
To find a truth already known:
What I love and really care for
I have left in England's home.

THE MASEFIELD GUIDE TO TAKEAWAYS

Star of India in gleaming gold and red paint,
Maitre d' leads you to a palm-screened waiting place.
Here you will receive your telephoned order,
Served in wicker hamper by a smiling face.

Noisy High Street *Chinky* with the TV blaring,
Orders on the counter and a queue outside.
Shouting from the kitchen as the woks are clashing,
Bags you 17, 33 and 45.

Plastic drive-away on the route to the suburbs –
Flashing neon signs shine on polystyrene trays –
Here they'll feed you as you keep your engine running:
Cola, Woppa Burgers and American Fries.

Dirty back street chip shop with its old oil smoking,
Slappy, with his dewdrop, batters fish and flies –
Sniffing, he'll serve you: flat fish, cod roe, fish cakes,
Jumbos, curry sauce and chips with grey meat pies.

FROM THE FAMILY ALBUM

Flanked by large carcasses and cuts,
forbears pose stiffly for the lens
below my Mother's maiden name
emblazoned on their butcher's shop.

The sign says, *Lapington & Son* –
his mutton chops beside the beef;
her bonnet, apron pristine white –
but of the son there is no sign.

Life in a bottle brought him down,
this black sheep who soon got the chop –
his birthright lost, a fortune gone,
the shop sold off by maiden aunts.

They, in their turn, gave all away
to feed the dogs at Battersea,
ensuring devil's progeny
would not receive life on a plate.

LAYING A GHOST

Phoebus completes his daily climb:
fingers of sunlight creep between
low cloud and mountains' top-most ridge –
steal down to wake the shaded town.
A sea mist shrouds Vesuvius;
where sun meets sea, a ferry glints.

The *Grand Hotel* beyond the town
presses her back against the cliff –
Reception's not at the front door
but five floors up via mirrored lift.
Her terraces and balconies
command a panoramic view

across the bay, across the town –
even the tiered swimming pool
looks out to sea from off the roof.
Shutters are raised, curtains undrawn –
the morning staff begin their shift –
as pampered guests greet a new dawn.

The sound of traffic starts to rise
from *Via Capo* far below,
the scooter hordes are just a drone,
lost in the sound of breakfast time.
Suave waiters in pristine *DJs*
adjust white linen, set the tone.

Coffee is served. I take a tour
around the striking breakfast bar:
a vast array of breads and fruit,
cereals, cheese, yoghurt and jams...
An omelette from *Short Order Chef*
is what I choose – loaded with ham.

The hot plates offer more delights,
there are mushrooms and tomatoes...
Small sausages next catch my eye,
mistaken for chipolatas,
I spoon them on, then take my plate
back to my seat in windowed sun.

Sorrento stretches out below,
the sea has turned an azure blue –
I watch a white boat sailing in
and marvel at the sparkling bay.
I toast *"Good luck"* with orange juice,
begin my breakfast, start my day.

I try a sausage - take a bite...
And I become a boy again,
transported back to family home.
All of the intervening years
become an insubstantial dream –
how quickly fifty disappear...

I'm sitting on a kitchen stool,
my Father's busy at the stove –
it's sausages, this Sunday's treat,
garlic for expatriate Pole.
"You like them? They are very good" –
he serves them up, loading my plate.

Later, in church, I'm feeling sick –
The heat and incense make me faint.
Embarrassed, I am led outside
where I can sit and breathe fresh air.
Joined by old ladies in the porch,
Water is brought to clear my head.

Is this a sign of growing old? –
memories haunt me every day.
A taste, a touch, a sight or sound
Can set me off in this strange way...

I finish off my sausages
And lay a ghost from far away.

THERE'S NO ACCOUNTING FOR TASTE
(HAIKU)

Cobwebs – Cassie's treat,
She hunts spider's tracery –
My cat's candyfloss.

GIANTS

They came, skimming our chimney pots,
one summer day when we were out –
just reaching to the field beyond.
Our startled neighbour told us how
she'd watched transfixed, holding her breath,
as wickerwork just cleared the roof.

This morning they were back again
on driest, calmest day for weeks:
when sun burnt off the valley's mist
and set damp cobwebs glittering.

I opened doors for cool fresh air
but caught a growing, roaring sound –
a giant's panting laboured breath.
A fiery red face glowered down
to billow over field-edged oak.

For seconds it stood quite erect,
towering over house and tree
then nylon rippled and collapsed
to stubble field, descends from skies:
colossus, creeping down to rest.

Ants seemed to pull a giant low
and roll away the canopy –
packing the basket with his face.
Now, they must wait for transport home:
their day over, mine just begun.

AND THE BEAT GOES ON...

We inched our way through edgy Camden crowds,
Avoiding broken glass and shouting men,
Until we found our refuge in the church.
Encamped on shabby chairs we settle in,
In silence waiting for our turn to speak –
Like alcoholics at their monthly meet.

Relaxed by wine, with readings now half through,
The crowd had warmed: expansive with applause,
Approving of the poems readers choose.
While quietly a woman read her verse
With audience straining hard to catch her words,
The street door at the rear noisily creaked,
Admitting fumes and noise from outside's world.

The door was quickly shut and peace regained –
But with a stranger now inside the hall.
Like flotsam, washed in on that sea of noise,
He seemed a refugee from urban sprawl.
Dishevelled, wrapped in layers of grimy clothes,
He clutches close his precious carrier bags
Whilst, ticket-less, he blags a place to sit.

No sooner is he in, than he's at home,
Unpacking manuscripts from plastic bags
And setting out his books on empty seats.
To some surprise he's called up to the stage
Where he's announced and suddenly things fit,
Can it be true, this frail and unkempt man
Was friend of Ginsberg, leader of the *Beats*.

As soon as he performed the penny dropped:
It *was* the man we'd seen so long ago,
The youngsters in the audience got a shock
When he became both chorister and bird.
Two poems and too quickly he was through,
The stage now given back to mortal men,
It's strange to be transported to the past,
To feel sixteen, and back in class again.

GOOD FRIDAY

Beneath sad skies and gently falling rain,
the only sound the joyous song of birds
on air so still no breath of wind can stir
the late spring trees unfurling fresh green leaves.

A charm of finches flashes gold and red
towards the valley where hedged blackthorn blooms;
up on the hill, wet glazes plough's fine tilth
and cowslips thrive beneath the plum and pear.

A slick of oil washes down the lane,
rain heals gouged verge where dying nettles lie,
a shattered grill and glass spill from the ditch
near scattered flowers from a last "goodbye."

WHEN AMBER LEFT

She left behind a trail of glinting light.
Marking each place where she had stepped, sequins
Shine up like tiny sparkling jewels from mats,
Carpet and chairs. Shed with each dancing step,

Each twirl, each laugh, it was the magic trail
From Disney's fairy wands —flashing down
To trace her joy in this new *princess* dress —
The one she hoped the Easter Bunny'd bring.

It's true the label warned, *Decorations*
May detach when washed—but not from joyous
Prancing... Like Cinderella I sweep up
And watch my busy *Dyson*'s innards gleam.

STALKER

Turning between the racks of clothes,
I pass a mirror - catch his eye –
in time to see him straightening up.

Careworn and stooped, he's here again,
his image in shop window panes,
and, looking older than before,
he leers from limousine's smoked glass.

At home I take him by surprise
when cornered in the smallest room,
I peer and catch his eye again –
reflect upon my father's face.

CONCESSIONS

Posh *Ralph* and *Calvin*
demanded a move:
"Away from all those
rough boys : Ted and *Ben..*
And all those Dockers" -
They just couldn't *Hackett.*

VIEWS FROM THE TOWPATH

Still waters reflect tall buildings,
cool, dark shadows under bridges,
reversed graffiti from old walls.

There's buddleia and willow herb,
moorhens and a heron fishing:
all of them in mirror image,
enlivening old watercourse.

To the side of the main channel
near a lock - quite unexpected -
is a pool of water lilies,
numbers doubled by reflections.

So exquisite in their setting -
walkers stop in admiration,
conversation turns to Monet's
Giverny - his water garden
and *Le Bassin Aux Nympheas...*

When does art become investment?
Do some eyes behold just money?
Can it still be "truth is beauty"
and, for all, that "beauty's truth?"

Here the sun still shines on water
highlighting these perfect lilies;
witness to Damascus moment
for a walker on the towpath,
pausing, on the way to Limehouse.

In June 2008, Claude Monet's painting **Le Bassin Aux Nympheas,** *was sold at auction in London for £41million.*

A KHANTY ELDER REMEMBERS

After the reindeer herds had left,
came Surgut to Siberia –
the fall-out from its oilfields
would turn the daytime into night.
And when, in wintertime, it snowed,
the broken landscape turned to soot...
and rare, indeed, were flakes of white.

So we imagined a white world
where trillions of snowflakes fell –
and only one as black as jet.
Unusual and beautiful,
this freak of nature, strange paillette,
was found and treasured like a pearl...
In Surgut, in our pristine world.

STRANGE BUT TRUE

Sometimes a life is strange but true:
A man who had a heart attack
Had fixed the hospital machine
Minutes before it saved his life.

But sometimes a strange life is true:
An undertaker short on trade
Came up with this surprising plan -
Free services on Christmas Day.

A life is true but sometimes strange:
A dog, missing on holiday,
Had somehow walked five hundred miles
To drive away his owner's grief.

But a true life is sometimes strange:
Libraries in the USA
Tried something quite unusual -
The *Playboy* magazine in Braille.

Strange life is sometimes a true *but*:
The smallest player on the field
out jumped a man of six feet one
To score - helped by *The Hand of God.*

Sometimes a life is strange but true:
The Post Office had sent a note explaining
Badly damaged mail -
This item was attacked by snails.

A life is true but sometimes strange:
The Headmaster of St. John's, Churt
Used his false leg to beat a boy
Who danced the maypole in reverse.

But a true life is sometimes strange:
Irish labourers went on strike
At a McAlpine building site
When issued boots marked *left* and *right.*

So, all in all, life can be strange -
Trying to pinpoint what is true -
I crave each fresh consistency
Like hearing you say *I love you.*

With acknowledgements to **True Stories** by Christopher Logue.

SURPRISE

Sometimes the unexpected is contrived –
For pure effect: the billboard mounted car,
The family house impaled by giant shark
Or scale *Titanic* dwarfing urban yards.
But then there is the genuine surprise:
Lonely piano on a mountain side
Or quiet grassy lane with blackthorn hedge
Where somebody has left a pristine fridge;
Here's perfect pram left on a gleaming beach
And pyre of stiff legged cows behind the hedge,
But worst – the arm that waves from shredded pines,
Marking this bomber's one and only time...

GOLDFINCHES

Exotics, on dull Lenten days,
outflank drab sparrows' dismal show
with tinkling, bell-like calls in flight
and flash of gold as off they go –
a charm of finches bob the hedge.

Pushed to the margins of the farms
where tractors spray with herbicides,
goldfinches seek untended scenes
for spiky teasels, thistledown
and groundsels' tiny wind-blown seeds.

Kept as a charm against the plague,
then caged for beauty and for song,
they almost died out in the wild
till keeping them was seen as wrong
and Parliament came to their aid.

Yet, down the ages they've appeared
in pictures of the infant Christ:
companions for a tiny child,
as symbols of the sacrifice
and passion that was yet to come...

These sweet-voiced, gold-winged tiny birds
pulled out the thorns to free Christ's crown.
In doing so, his blood was spilled
and blessed them with a love profound –
marking cheeks red as sacred birds.

TOWARDS WINTER

WORLD'S BIGGEST MORTGAGE BAIL OUT
All stay in the red:
Blackberries in the hedgerow
Blend with hips and haws.

CRIME AND RACIAL TENSION WILL SOAR IN SLUMP
Grown tall these wild trees,
Apples now too high to reach,
Fruit rots in the lane.

WALL ST. CRISIS TO ROCK MARKETS
Littering the path,
Fresh green cones stripped to the core:
Squirrel's autumn treat.

BANKS UNDER SIEGE
Flocks of pigeons wheel,
Tracking grain spilled on the ground,
Perch on haystacked corn.

BANK IS BLOWN AWAY
Sky like a sundae:
Crushed blackberries stain cream clouds,
Orange juices run.

FAILED BANK CHIEF IS £200M WINNER
Cobwebs glint with dew
Birdsong greets a golden dawn,
Hostas' green turns gold.

BRADFORD & BINGLEY FALL PREY TO CREDIT CRUNCH
Acorns are falling.
Young jays calling from the trees
Add to secret store.

BRITAIN'S £150 BN "TOXIC BANK"
Gunfire from the copse:
Heron, crows, rooks, pigeons, geese –
The whole field rising.

STARING INTO THE ABYSS
Before the rains came:
Six butterflies in the sun,
Dance at summer's wake.

MARKET MAYHEM
Dawn. An owl flies home
Low, over the motorway –
Just makes it this time.

HEADLINES: 01/09/08 – 07/10/08

LOOKING BACK

And now's the time to make the journey back,
To pack your bag and set off down the track.
Will you head for the station's slow train west?
Or would a flight from Heathrow suit you best?

A package tour by coach does not seem right;
A limo trip would mean you'd miss the sights.
You know, you've still got time to catch the boat,
...And time in hand to plan for life afloat.

However, you'll be governed by the tide,
So don't delay too long while you decide
Forget the harvest moon and stars so bright
As now's the time to sail – tonight's the night!

Remember, long ago when setting out
How youth's excitement submerged every doubt?
Don't falter now, cast off and keep on track,
The only way is forward – looking back.

LILIES of the VALLEY

At four or five they gave to me
A bed of Granddad's un-worked land
Between the shed and garden path
And end-stopped by the water butt.

The old man helped me dig and plant.
Next Spring I watched the leaves unfurl,
The buds break into tiny bells
That turned from green to arctic white.

I was excited – pleased as punch –
The day the flowers made a show,
Ready for bed, I scampered out
Bursting with pride for one last look.

A thrush sang from the lilac blooms -
I couldn't name the bird or tree –
I only knew that beauty's found
In birdsong, sun, sweet fragrances.

Hearing my name, I straightened up
From land I've planted and reclaimed;
Somehow the evening has moved on
With all the shadows lengthening...

I gather up pyjamaed son,
Wondering where the time has gone.

A RUNNER'S PASSING

He rose to shut the window tight
Against the slanting rain
And paused to watch a runner pass –
Go splashing down the lane
Near the stables and the farmhouse
And the crop of dripping grain.

Frowzy with sleep, he rubbed his eyes
To take in this dawn rite:
The fields were still and no bird sang
In grey and watery light –
But yellow vest bobbed steadily
Downhill and out of sight.

He thought of all the miles he'd trained
In rain and frost and sun,
How his obsession governed him –
Each day he had to run –
But now, in age, it's back to bed...
His rest day just begun.

PRIVET

...I cannot like the scent,
Yet I would rather give up others more sweet,
With no meaning, than this bitter one
(Old Man – Edward Thomas)

Initially, like Thomas's "*Old Man,*"
this pungent smell is difficult to place:
familiar – both bitter and yet sweet –
it does not chime with me like other scents.

Hovering on thick air like memories,
it stops me in my tracks and makes me think:
arriving in fresh waves, just like the past,
it leads me to a hedge across the street.

Carefully shaped : dark leaves cut trim and close,
do not disclose the very thing I seek
but, where the shears have missed a growing tip,
tiny white spikes of flowers now persist.

There, softly in late sun, scent speaks to me:
transports me down the vista of the years
to where an old man, dressed in corduroy,
flashes quick shears, watched by a lonely boy.

VILLANELLE

For an Action Man's 70ᵗʰ Birthday

Now charge your cup, drink up your wine –
the last wine at the feast is best...
You're feeling good and in your prime,
but there's no need to walk the line
or look out for another quest,
so charge your cup, drink up your wine.
No one's suggesting writing rhyme
from rose-trimmed cottage in the west –
we *know* you're good and in your prime!
Stop looking round for things to climb,
you've stayed the course and passed the test:
now charge your cup, drink up your wine.
A holiday is not a crime –
we think it's time you took a rest –
we *know* you're good and in your prime!
With three score years and ten behind
blow out your candles, please your guests –
you're looking good and in your prime
so charge your cup, drink up your wine.

ON MY MIND

As usual, they are on my mind –
I wonder how they'll be today,
one fast asleep, will not see dawn,
the other, restless and confused,
is up and dressed by half past four
and ready to begin a day
of fitful snoozing in his chair.

Their frailties now weigh heavily:
just keeping them in their own home
is now the balance of my life.
Uncertain as an accident,
one trip or fall crossing the room
will be enough to change it all –
making their lives impossible.

Now everywhere the everyday
is set beside them like a trap:
a boiling kettle, heated pan,
are booby-traps for shaky hands.
A shelf becomes a stretch too far –
while *Use By* dates, deep in the fridge,
will baffle their uncertain sight.

Waking at four, escaping dreams,
my day starts in the usual way:
worries, about the coming year,
unveil themselves as it grows light.
Soon thoughts race on to Christmastide –
a gleam of hope at this dark time
when we take strength from seasons past...

And still a single, brilliant star
shines from the frosty, eastern sky.

OUT OF THE KITCHEN

In the kitchen, redundant and unused,
cookery books still line the dusty shelves.
Your prized mixer's not stirred a cake in years
and carers microwave your lunch at twelve.

Tidying your larder, clearing the jam
of tins and jars that we have found too late,
I discover your hoard of bottled plums,
now out of reach...and sight...and mind...and date.

Red-gold of autumn, captured in those jars
remind me of an afternoon of rain:
baskets of Blaisdons, saucepans on the stove...
A pleasure you will never take again.

GETTING PAST IT

There's something sad
in an aged Don Juan
whose looks are gone.

And a fighting man
turns from champ to chump
when his brain's punch-drunk.

Now this ageing mum
finds it hard to think –
simply, memory
is on the blink...
In her easy chair
with her cup of tea –
seems she's forgetting
both you and me.
It's sad she has lost
all the things we shared :
cannot remember
how much we care...

She is stripped of all
that she used to be
and in her eyes
it's plain to see
she has gone beyond
all the things she's known –
could be anywhere,
now she's lost at home –
she mutters sad prayers
to her God above...
keeping her alive
is just faith... and love.

VALENTINE

Do you remember courting grebes? –
Seen from the towpath down near Sonning.
Early that year, despite the cold,
a romance timed for Valentine's –
a bonding both on bank and river :
the watching couple and the birds.
Today I offer you my heart...
and constancy, like courting grebes.

PARTING

And when we kissed and shared our tears,
into my hand she pressed a heart:
a silver locket to keep safe –
a token of her lasting love.

Later, and many miles away,
I cherished it and thought of her:
its tiny chamber velvet blue
and empty... but my heart was full.

FRESH FIGS

The best way to eat figs is from the tree
when ripe, pendulous, breast-like fruit hangs down –
just weigh them in your hands and gently squeeze
and take them, nearly bursting, soft and brown.

Like gynaecologists some slice each fig,
halving the ripe fruit with such precision,
they scoop the inside out with shiny spoons –
spend ages contemplating each incision.

I think the Turkish Figs are best caressed:
you take them, holding stalk end at the top,
then gently slide a finger down below
to open up that tender honey spot.

Next, gently prise soft fleshiness apart
exposing that moist pinkness to your tongue,
enjoy yourself as honeyed juices flow
into your mouth and down your chin it runs...

Like Pavlov's dog, when figs come into view,
I always seem to conjure thoughts of you.

THE BEST DAYS

At two o'clock this morning
I lay thinking of your smile,
Of all our times together
Down the years, across the miles;
Of days we were first lovers –
How you made me feel complete –
Waiting so impatiently
Till next when we could meet.

In poems and in letters
And promises I made you
I remember all the ways
Your love has touched my life
Memories of yesterdays
And dreams of great tomorrows,
Promises we made and all
The best days of my life...

We shared some tears and sunshine
As we watched our children grow;
Remembered strange adventures
And some times when life seemed slow.
We rode on stormy waters
And saw out long foggy days –
I believe the love we share
Can never fade away.

In poems and in letters
And promises I made you
I remember all the ways
Your love has touched my life
Memories of yesterdays
And dreams of great tomorrows,
Promises we made and all
The best days of my life...

TO THE SPLENDOUR, TO THE PAST

Couple arm in arm, sticks at either end,
Are slower now than fifty years ago:
Down alleyways and creeping round the bends,
Their hearts go back to when they weren't so slow.

They're here in Venice making last *"goodbyes"* –
In final sunset and that afterglow –
Now every bridge becomes a *Bridge of Sighs*
As palaces tinge pink for just a while.

The glory of the *Doge* against the sky
Made crossing *St. Mark's Square* seem like a mile.
At *Florian* they stopped to rest outside,
Rejoicing in the splendour and the style.

As darkness falls they reach the waterside,
Await gondola and their final ride.

DARK

As life's a bitch I worry about time
And seek enough to endure my small pain:
To see my words dance in a glowing line,
Turn into verse that proudly bears my name.

When looking up into a clear blue sky
I trace the jet trails high above the strand,
And wonder if I'll ever live to share
The magic and romance of distant lands.

Then thinking, my sweet lady, of the day
That's sure to come when I see you no more,
Never again delighting in your ways
Or with your perfect love to rest secure –

At fate's lousy joke, I'll laugh if I can –
Life happens when you're busy making plans.

TRISTRAM and ISEULT

How will you know me when I'm far away?
In the voice of the blackbird, in the first light of day.

My hands wave unseen in the shimmering leaves
But I'll whisper "I love you," on the breath of a breeze.

Remember my essence in the scent of a rose
As you feel my touch where the cool waters close.

Picture my smile in the warm ember's glow
And soon I will greet you with the kiss of the snow.

COUPLE

Theirs, not some meteoric rise
That in no time just flared and fell -
A rocket bursting from the skies,
Plummeting to a tabloid hell.

Nor like some joy ride fuelled by lust,
Reckless, racing out of control -
A photo flash, a plume of dust -
Before the final skid and crash.

More like an accident at sea:
They run aground on unmarked rocks
Then drift and float expectantly
Hoping to find a palm-fringed life ...

Steering towards that western gleam,
Clutching the wreckage of their dreams.

CONDITIONAL

How his heart bleeds:
Regardless of however much he pleads,
She still cries, "No!"
And says, "If you don't like it, you can go."

She loved him most
The day his bonus cheque came in the post,
Now he sighs, "No!"
And says, "If you don't like it, you can go."

A GARDENER'S LOST LOVE

Ancient legends say
they sprang from bitter tears,
petals red with lover's blood
when Aphrodite grieved.

Grown near border's edge,
he brushed them as he passed;
stopped close by to field her call –
admired them as she laughed.

Nodding in the breeze,
they seemed to share his grief:
her last words burnt in his mind –
betrayed beyond belief.

Ordering more plants,
his catalogue spells out:
Love-lies-bleeding, Love-in-a-mist,
Anemone: Lost love.

Lost Love	- Anemone Coronaria
Love-lies-bleeding	- Amaranthus Caudatus
Love-in-a-mist	- Nigella Damascena

SONG FOR ...

You need to get things straight –
agreed between you two;
you have to put things right in your lives,
you need to see things through.

How did the good times end?
Where did the closeness go?
You've got to get things back on track
before some real tears flow...

CHORUS:

Please don't turn and walk away
before the talking starts –
you need to head for the light,
you've got to make this thing right.

You must come up with a way
to give each other a say:
watch the storm clouds disappear
by the end of the day...

Somewhere at the rainbow's end
you'll find the way to start:
you need to make it come true –
don't ever say that you're through.

CHORUS:

Please don't turn and walk away
before the talking starts –
you need to head for the light,
you've got to make this thing right.

You need to get things straight –
agreed between you two –
you have to put things right in your lives,
you have to see things through.

You've got to get things back on track
ignite that precious spark:
you've got to make this thing right,
you've got to make this thing right...

HUMAN SHIELD

We all know that old baddies' trick:
grabbing the girl, shouting, *"Keep back!"*
escaping with a human shield –
a coward with the upper hand
who's vanquished by the final reel.
But sadly, real life's not like that:
sometimes the heroine will die,
the wicked triumph - mocking good –
and children will be used as pawns.

The Nazis on their Eastern Front,
the Middle East, Afghanistan
had citizens used like a wall:
a shield for gunmen, troops and bombs.
Western ex-pats shielded Saddam
and Taliban used their own kind
to by-pass justice, cross the line...

More tricky than the Taliban? –
Some middle-class, Home Counties wives.
Idle, indulged, these self-obsessed
have never had to work a stroke:
large house, new car and help with chores
are good returns for doing *nowt.*
And when they get bored with their lives –
decide a change will do them good –
their first thought is this sinecure:
to have it all by hook or crook.

Hiding behind their kids, they say
no one could bear what they've endured;
directing *fatwahs* through the courts
they geld, then shackle husbands' lives.
They claim mild spouses were like beasts
and how, for their poor children's sake
they stole away... (without the guts
to mention what was in their thoughts).

Shocked husbands never had a chance:
the one-eyed, gender-biased courts
will pick these suckers to the bone –
motives and truth, it seems, don't count –
kid's welfare must, of course, come first
and so men lose the family home,
their pensions and their hard-earned cash.

There are no winners in this game
though dice are loaded from the start,
these selfish women fail to see
that what they did broke children's hearts
and they will lose more than they gained
when kids rebel and then depart.

ZIPPED

We're missing you - it makes us sigh
to hear so little news of you:
don't let this stand-off mean "*Goodbye.*"

It's good to talk - at least to try -
too many people now feel blue...
one day you'll realise why they cry.

Your fear of being "*Analysed*" -
becomes a fear of facing truth:
should your cool stand-off mean "*Goodbye?*"

So much was changed by natty lies -
we only wanted what was true -
not seeing you just makes us sigh.

To keep your friendships, don't be shy:
just tell it straight, give us a clue -
a tight-lipped silence means "*Goodbye.*"

If we could help to clarify
the things that you've declared taboo,
perhaps we wouldn't have to sigh...
perhaps there would be no "*Goodbye.*"

PICTURE THIS...

This is a picture: not a little one
In my colouring book,
Not a painting, like I do at school,
This one is special –
On a big, big sheet of card...
And I shall colour carefully,
Not going over any lines
With my new, best pens.
I've made this special picture big
To put in all the happy times:
Here's the zoo and over there the sea,
My sister on her bike,
Our house by those tall trees,
A sparkly princess dress,
My best friend, Emily
And Mummy when she always laughed...
Over here – by the black bit –
There's room to put my Dad,
One day soon when he comes back
I'll show him, then he won't be sad...

The doorbell rings – "Who's at the door?"
"It's Emily come round to play."
I'll stop, put on my princess dress
...And finish this another day.

DRESSING THE TREE

Like Scrooge's knocker on his door,
a lion mask surveys the scene
from high upon the Inn's front wall.
Here, in the ancient heart of town,
a crowd fills up the Market Square
to stand beneath the Christmas lights
and mark the dressing of the tree.

Dads, late from work, meet family groups
to watch as baubles, made in schools,
are raised by a triumphant Mayor.
Cameras flash and choirs sing
as trimmings soon are hauled aloft –
raised safely by hard-hatted men
who cherry-pick each bauble's spot
where they will gleam and gently swing.

United, whilst their youngest child
had led the choir, sung out her heart,
this family starts their war again.
While others queue for hot mince pies,
by diverse routes they leave the square:
father, sad kids, mother elsewhere –
by Christmas they will live apart...

And, from the tip of this year's tree,
a sad-eyed moon sees everything:
Waxing to wane, waxing to wane.

THIN PICKINGS

The day broke from a purple east –
cloud building for the Equinox –
a late owl, hazy crescent moon
were there to share St. Stephen's feast.

My birthday gifts of ice and snow
still gripped us through till Christmas Day:
cancelled my celebration meal,
as blocked roads kept my guests away.

For days the garden's hungry birds
fluttered and jostled in their need
at feeders hanging from the wall
whilst others scavenged ground for seed.

Thin pickings for the nervous rat,
driven by hunger to compete
with chaffinch, blackbird and the rest –
I tapped cold glass...a brief retreat.

Like refugees from frozen fields,
a flock of redwings stopped to feed
unnoticed on the roundabout
by harassed shoppers, Christmas Eve.

And all this time a fretful child,
worried that she had no fixed home,
is passed from Mum to Dad and back –
will she find Christmas on her own?

LAST MAN STANDING
(i.m. Harry Patch 17/06/1898 - 25/07/09)

The bugle sounds, the flags unfurl
in memory of a modest man
whose life was haunted by a dream
of clinging mud and fearful noise.

He'd heard the cries of injured men
while being marched to Pilchem Ridge,
then crawled through mud, turned red by blood,
and, to a random shell, lost friends.

He said that war was nothing more
than murder by another name –
this last man from that fading band
who fought at Ypres and Passchendaele.

The nation saw him as a link
to multitudes who gave their lives :
a living emblem for the lost –
an icon to be eulogised.

But Harry Patch eschewed his fame –
despised the glorying of war;
"It's just showbiz...Remembrance Day" –
he hated pomp and ritual.

A soldier's send-off held at Wells –
but he'd not want an ornate tomb,
reluctant hero to the end
he'll rest in peace at Monkton Combe.

POPPIES

They fell amongst the poppies there,
in Flanders Fields in Passchendaele;
we promised to remember them :
their war to end all wars.

Today, amongst the poppy fields
of Helmand in Afghanistan,
young soldiers still give up their lives –
it seems we never learn.

And, as we lay our poppy wreaths,
a bitter harvest far away
will help destroy our youth today –
a hidden kind of war.

DRAGON'S TEETH

...So, to his next task, Jason turned.
He set about to plant the field
and, where the dragon's teeth were sown,
a phantom army sprang to life:

each man a soldier, fully armed,
and ready to take up the fight.
To beat them single-handedly
was far too much for any man,

but Jason knew he would prevail
and, working to Medea's plan,
from cover (hidden by a bush)
into the field he hurled large stones.

Each man he struck became incensed,
accusing neighbours of attack -
and in no time a battle raged:
red mist, hot blood...into the black.

Another field - Afghanistan -
where dragon's teeth, by Taliban,
are sown in every village there.
Our modern Jasons, Daves and Johns

Are truly brave and just as strong
as any of those Ancient Greeks...
yet battle on with no real plan -
Medea's cunning is not theirs.

Insurgents, like a rising tide,
spring up across the countryside:
there seems to be an extra man
for every fallen Taliban.

This is a war that can't be won:
no golden apples of the sun,
no black gold or a trophy fleece -
just politicians in retreat.

JUPITER
August 24th, 79 A.D.

Approaching Hurculaneum,
a whiff of sulphur on the breeze
and, high above Vesuveus,
that monstrous cloud shaped like a tree.
The darkness of the falling ash
engulfed the land along the coast,
but as we sailed into the port
thin ash that fell here was like smoke.
"Old Hercules protects his own,"
the Captain chuckled as we docked,
"He's sent his wrath to purge Pompeii," -
but how I wished we'd stayed afloat.

Later, on land, I felt the shocks -
like some strange wind below the ground -
rumbling down towards the dock,
making the villas shake like leaves.
A thunder crack - a wave of heat
like opening a furnace door -
as sky turned dark and hard rain fell.
The people stumbled to the beach,
covered in ash and white as ghosts,
to wait until the earthquake passed
like many had in childhood.

We sheltered in the warehouses -
the air was thick and hot as hell -
while pumice rained down on the beach:
a grey scum clogging up the sea.
Deep in the warehouse, in the dark,
there came a crash, a flash of light -
just heat, no air ... My head explodes.

Sometimes I wonder where I am...
on looking out from where I lay
I see no sea - the beach has gone –
I look out on a rocky wall.
It's strange to see how much has changed –
bare ruins seem familiar –
I recognise much of this town
but not the jostling foreign crowds –
What do they seek? Where are they from?

On days like these I sense the sea
and wish that I could sail away,
back home towards Neapolis –
shatter these ties that bind to me...

JUPITER : equivalent to "Thursday" in the Roman calendar.
JUPITER (Jove) was the supreme god of Roman mythology. He determined
human affairs and made known the future through signs and portents.

PRESENCE
(At Barbara Hepworth's Trewyn Studios and Museum, St. Ives.)

They should place a sign here reading
"*Back in five minutes.*" Here as left,
your work smocks hang behind the door,
tools still lie where they were dropped - work
has only briefly stopped. It may
be luck - or artifice, perhaps -
but it's as if you've slipped away.
"*Gone out for lunch*" or "*Popped next door*"
are messages we might expect
left propped against your last maquette.

Gone thirty years and more... it's true,
yet all seems well and life means all
it ever meant. Out of sight can
never mean you're out of mind. Your
garden flourishes as planned, where
mute sculptures stand as monuments
to talent and to taste. And could
it be the same for everyone -
to slip away as you have done?
to tantalise and seemingly
to wait so close: ephemeral
as scent on air; in the next room
perhaps, somewhere about the house?

Indigo Dreams Publishing
132, Hinckley Road
Stoney Stanton
Leicestershire
LE9 4LN
www.indigodreams.co.uk